How To Start an

Apparel Business

James Taylor

From the Desk James Moore Editor of Bull City Publishing:

Dear Friend,

If at Any point while you're reading this book you have any questions, please don't hesitate to contact us. You can best reach us at Twitter (@bullcitypub), or on our Facebook Fan Page

Even if you don't have any questions, We'd love for you to come by and say hello! If you want to reach us in a private you can email us at info@bullcitypublishing.com or on our blog Bullcitypublishing.com/blog

Warmest Regards,

James Moore

Editor & Chief, Bull City Publishing, LLC

Do you Love Reading? Do you want a Ton of FREE Kindle Books? Join our Mailing list by emailing us at **freebooks@bullcitypublishing.com**

TABLE OF CONTENT

Introduction

Just like starting any new business, to start an apparel business, you must have the desire and passion to fully devote yourself in one of the most dynamic and competitive marketing proposition of today. Though not recommended, but it's highly suggested to have a vocational qualification in the field of fashion designing or retail marketing, to help you equipped with the desired confidence and mindset to compete with other apparel businesses. Eventually, the most important quality for a business owner who intends to start and survive an apparel business is creativity and a great fashion sense, so that you are able to cater to the real needs of the people at large, i.e. coming up with what they want and not just filling your store with undesirable junk.

Following are some of the tips in this regard, that can really help you making a suitable business plan for starting your own apparel business -

The first plan for a startup would be to decide about the types of apparels to be sold in the store. The best thing a startup can do is to focus on single line of apparels i.e. it can be exclusive for men or exclusive for women or exclusive for kids only. Reason for same is that, to sell apparels for all ages and genders you need to have more investments, extensive knowledge and expertise in terms of marketing different segments of clothes and more manpower to manage high inventories of clothes.

Further, a startup business that intends to sell any one particular niche of apparels can even start his initial business from a spare space of your house or one that belongs to your friend or family. It's an easy way to save on paying huge amount of advance fee and monthly rentals required in hiring a shop space. In case of sufficient investment available, a better business space can be opted.

Next is to decide for a unique and easy name for your apparel business but remember, it's always better to have a short and crisp business name having all the potential of getting distinctively popular with its clients. Once a business name is decided, then you have to obtain the necessary permissions or licenses, as required to run an apparel store. This may include the sales tax number and value added tax number, etc.

The idea is to ensure that all legal compliances are satisfactory met.

Now it's time to have tie-ups with the wholesalers or the manufactures that are dealing in range of apparels to be sold at your store. This way you can have best of bargains and variety of clothes available for sale. You can also think of having franchisee tie-ups with big brands that also helps in setting up display infrastructure for your store. Benefit of having a franchisee tie-up is that you become a part of the aggressive and effective marketing campaign with better brand awareness that a franchisee enjoys. It must be remembered that there are certain franchisee fees and profit sharing agreements, which you have to agree with. It's always to know the pros and cons of such franchisee tie-up and business opportunities that you can avail by dedicating such extra investment.

Another important aspect of planning for an apparel business today is to take into consideration the online competition that is posing huge threat to the apparels businesses. To cope up with this competition, you have to come up with great ways of on-the-counter display of products, along with a pleasing appearance of infrastructure that would help attracting more and more buyers. This also needs for having the latest and the reasonable range of apparels being displayed and sold, to cater to the needs of buyers who wish to physically feel the product before buying it. Eventually, you have to be dynamic and responsive to the needs of the buyers of your area.

Having finished with above activities, you have to then look after providing various sales and delivery options. This includes - option to buy online, home delivery of products, multiple paying options such as payment by credit card, payments in EMIs etc., to attract more and more customers. Having an easy exchange or return option, which would help the customers to buy more with ease. You can also provide various offers like membership cards with loyalty discounts on further purchases, cash back or discount coupons etc., which could prove sale boosters and help adding returning customers to your business. Rest assured that the above said initiatives coupled with excellent after-sales services; you can really give delight services to your customers. Always remember that, nothing could do better than the word of mouth advertisement, as received from your satisfactory clients.

Finally, you have to create brand awareness about your apparel store through flyers, leaflets and advertisement campaigns undertaken in local media such as newspapers, yellow pages directories and visual displays made at public places. Also, do consider about the most important medium of advertisement today, which is the digital marketing done online. This medium requires you to have a personal website made for your store stating the unique selling points of your business along with the benefits that a customer can have while purchasing clothes from your apparel store. Social media marketing is an important part of the online marketing that helps in having loads of awareness for your products and getting more potential customers.

The above said business plan is an important ingredient to achieve success in any apparel business. Though the list is not exhaustive, it really depends on line of clothing that you choose to start with keeping in mind the needs and paying capacities of the people residing within the vicinity of your apparel business.

Part 1:

Starting Up Your Business

CHAPTER 1

Choosing Your Business Entity

One of the first and perhaps the most critical questions that you need to ask yourself before getting started with your business is – which is the right business entity for my business? If you have been able to answer this question well, you can hope to have an easy sail in the ocean of business opportunities. Choosing the right business entity can take you a long way in managing your business liability, taxes and operations.

*"Start where you are, use what you have, do what you can." – **Arthur Ashe***

Before you get started on choosing the right business entity, there are a few things that you need to consider and ponder a thought on. Firstly, you need to pay heed to the degree by which are liable for the organization's legal and financial risks. Another aspect of liability is the tax liability. You, as the owner, get to choose the layers of taxation and the process by which the same needs to be pursued. Besides this, the business entity chosen determines how well you can attract investors by showing them ownership interests and the operational costs required for maintaining the business.

Before we move on to discussing entity types, their advantages and their disadvantages, it is important for you to understand that your business will change and evolve over time. Therefore, there is no single appropriate entity type for a business. The right business type will change as the business type changes. The fundamental categorization used for describing entity types is the number of owners involved in the business. For instance, if there is only one owner in a business, then the business can be registered as a sole proprietorship, Limited Liability Company or a corporation. However, if the number of owners is higher than this number, the business can be registered as a limited liability company, corporation, limited liability partnership, limited partnership or a general partnership.

Sole Proprietorship

When there is only one owner in a business, then the business is usually registered as a sole proprietorship. In such a business entity, the business is same as the individual. All the legal and financial liabilities of the business lie with the individual who owns the business. Most startups begin as sole proprietorship, which makes it the commonest form of business entity type used.

The advantage of using this business type is that the operational costs involved in running corporations and companies can be avoided using this business type. In addition, the tax for the business needs to be submitted along with the tax of the individual. So, paying taxes for the businesses and managing finances is much simpler. However, where there are advantages, there are several disadvantages as well. Since it is a one-man show, all the liability of the business lies with the owner. Therefore, there is no liability protection.

Corporation

When there are many owners or partners involved in a business, it is necessary that the business be created as a separate entity, which has a completely separate taxation, legal and financial structure. To address these needs of businesses as they grow, the business can be registered as a corporation. There are several classes of corporations and you can check on which one is the best for you by going through the local authority corporation formation manual.

Typically, the structure of a corporation is such that it includes three classes of people namely officers, directors and shareholders. The directors appoint officers while the shareholders elect the directors. The officers supervise all the major decisions concerned with the organization are taken by the directors and the day-to-day operations of the company.

There are several advantages of getting your business registered as a corporation. The fundamental advantage is the fact that there is liability protection and no one person can be held responsible for the financial and legal affairs of the business. Besides this, the ownership of the company can be transferred easily and may exist forever. There is no dependence on a single person for the existence of the business. Lastly, corporations allow shares to be sold and employee programs to be run under its name. The only disadvantage of such a formation, if at all it can be considered a disadvantage, is the fact that its operations and management is not as simple as that of its other counterparts. Since the formation entails several classes of management, meetings need to be held and a single person in the company can take no decision.

Limited Liability Company

This type of a business entity is a middle path between a corporation and a sole proprietorship. While it allows multiple people to hold stakes in a business and offer personal assets protection, it allows the simple taxation model used in sole proprietorship to be used by the owners of the company. A LLC is an extension of a sole proprietorship in the sense that it allows multiple owners. However, the liability of the business can be help by a member, management or team of officers. Therefore, registering your business as a LLC offers you higher flexibility. However, this may act against you as well in the sense that this is not a business entity that is liked and preferred by investors.

Partnerships

Apart from LLC, multiple owner businesses may also opt for a partnership. Three types of partnership entities exist. These types are general partnerships, limited partnerships and limited liability partnerships. Any partnership that involves two or more people in a business that is tied together with their interest in the profit that the business generates is treated as a general partnership. Since the members are directly associated with the profits and losses, there is no liability protection offered by this form of a business entity. However, where it does offer you relief is in the taxation process. You can easily get rid of the layered taxation using this business entity.

The second type of partnership is a limited partnership. In such a business formation, the partners in the business share liabilities. So, no single partner is liable for the business in full. This reduces the risk liable on each owner as well. The difference between a general partnership and a limited partnership is that the former may exist without any proper documentation as well. However, the later requires formal agreements and documentation. Lastly, limited liability partnerships are a business entity that is reserved for certain licensed professionals.

Which Is The Right Business Entity For Your Business?

Finalizing the right business entity for your business requires you to answer the following three questions:

- How many business owners are involved and who are they?

- What are the stakes of these business owners on the losses and profits of the business?

- How and when the business is expected to generate profits?

CHAPTER 2

Business Plan Basics

Before you start a business, one of the fundamental things that you will need to look at is how to get investors, banks and capitalists interested in your project. To pitch your businesses' potential to these key players, you will need to present a solid business plan to them. The three basic things that your plan must have are clarity of thought, focus and realism.

Apart from these, it must be clear from the plan itself that you have the resources, in terms of expertise and infrastructure to meet your objectives. In a way, the business plan must be able to communicate to the investors and everyone interested that you have the capability to put your words into action.

The relevance of a business plan doesn't end at getting financial support. A business plan is a 'plan' for you to follow and come back to every time you feel lost in your endeavor. It is a kind of roadmap to your business journey. Moreover, it is not a document that you will write once and keep in your office drawer. It is a document that you will need to go back to and edit it as and when required.

All in all, it is a document for you to reference, keep your focus right and meet deadlines. So, as your business evolves, the growth curve for your business plan will also show a corresponding growth.

Is A Business Plan Really Required?

Many businesses start without a business plan. So, having a business plan is not a mandatory requirement for starting a business. However, it is certainly a beneficial proposition to have a business plan to show to your investors and prospective partners. If you are hoping to get a bank loan, then a professionally made business plan is a must-have for you. Moreover, you will need it even if you have a running business and need a loan to expand it.

To summarize the reasons why you need a business plan and how having a business plan will come in handy for you in critical situations, the following pointers have been listed out.

- Define business objectives for your new venture

- Raise finances for business startup or expansion

- Review the progress of the business and correct the course and focus wherever required.

- Define the terms of agreements with investors and partners

- Outline all the financial and legal aspects of the business

- Evaluate and state all the aspects of the business in terms of promotion, expansion and growth.

What Should A Business Plan Include?

All in all, from the perspective of the reader, your business plan must show exactly and how you will generate revenue for your business and give the investors and a good return on their value. The fundamental components of a typical business plan include:

- **Executive Summary**

  This is a summary of your business plan and must outline all the important points of the plan in not more than a couple of pages.

- **Company Summary**

  This section must outline the details about your company, its objectives, history and goals.

- **Products/Services**

  This section must describe all the products and services that the company offers. In addition, this section must also describe how these products or services are better than the other products and services that exist in the market.

- **Market Analysis**

  This section explores everything about the market in terms of the customer base, competitors, and size of the market and how the market is expected to behave in the near and far future.

- **Strategy and Implementation**

  This section describes the strategy that you plan to implement for putting your plan into action. In addition, this section must also include details about milestones and deadlines.

- **Management Summary**

  An important aspect of consideration while evaluating business credentials is the team, management and staff that are involved. This section gives a detailed account of the management and team along with their experiences and achievements.

- **Financial Plan**

  This section includes all the financial details about the project in terms of profits and cash flows.

How To Write A Business Plan?

While you are busy setting up your business, taking the time out to sit in front of the computer and do all the required writing can be a daunting task. In fact, for many new businessmen, writing a business plan, as the first thing, can sound like a vicious loop that is impossible to get out of. The details that you may be expected to furnish, as part of the business may be too detailed for you predict, estimate and precisely state. To make the whole process easier for you, there are several alternatives that you may explore for a sail through this seemingly daunting process.

- **Hire Someone**

   The easiest thing to do is to outsource the whole process of writing a business plan to a professional. Although, the consultant will be there for you and will help you through the process, you will still need to think your business out and explain your goals and objectives to the consultant so that a good business plan can be created.

- **Read Books And Do Some Research**

   If hiring a professional doesn't seem like an affordable option for you, you may look through a few books and see if you can train yourself for the business plan creation process.

There are several books available in the market and you can look through any of them or look at some online sources for help.

- **Use A Specialized Software**

  If you feel that you can create a business plan, but starting the creation process from scratch may not feel like your thing to you, you may also look at some business planning software packages to help you get started easily and make the whole process more convenient.

How To Create A Perfect Business Plan?

Like we mentioned in the very beginning of this chapter, a successful business plan must have three main characteristics namely, clarity, realism and focus. Therefore, it is crucial that the business plan must be well thought out, precise, logical in structure, concise in the way it is written and communicate to the reader exactly how the team is competent enough to achieve the set goals and generate profit.

CHAPTER 3

Organizing A Corporation

Once the business has been formalized, you can expect to receive the formal agreements and documents concerned with the business. By the time you receive these documents, you must have all the organization steps done on your part. For instance, you will need to have the basic certificates, documents and minutes ready. We have included this information in this chapter to make the process easier for you.

Organizing Meeting

It is the responsibility of the company to hold a meeting in which all the directors of the company must be present. This meeting must ideally be conducted as early as possible. In this meeting, the directors must take some basic decisions like finalizing the top management, set the fiscal year, adopt seal and make decisions regarding banking arrangements.

Corporation's Books

It is the responsibility of the corporation to maintain a book at its registered office. This book must contain the following information: shareholders agreement, by-laws, articles, resolutions, minutes of the meeting, details of the present director including name and term details, details of the shareholders and the number of shares each of them holds and the amount of money that each share has due on it.

Shareholders to have a look at the information can access this book. However, they cannot access director information and information about the resolutions and meetings. Only auditors and directors can access this information. If at all, the shareholders need to access this information, they will need to take permission from the director. This is mentioned in the shareholders agreement. In addition, the shareholders may also take the permission of the director to gain access to by-laws, articles and shareholders agreement.

Corporation's Registers

The corporation's minute book has various registers. Upon organization of the company, these registers must be completed in full.

Director's Registers

This is a register that contains all the details about all the directors who have attained office. Along with the names of the registers, the addresses and personal details of the directors are given. Besides this, details about when a director assumed office and the details of when the term ended or the when the term is ending are also present in this book.

Shareholder's Register

Every corporation has a list of shareholders along with their personal details and the shares that they hold. In addition, other details like when the individual became a shareholder and date at which the shareholder gave up his or her shares, if the individual is no longer a shareholder, are also shared in this register.

Share Register

This register has an alphabetical list of all the shareholders and the list of shares they possess. In addition, other details about of the shares are also given, which include date of purchase, certificate number, price per share, total amount of money that the shareholder paid and the total number of shares that the shareholder owns.

Share Transfer Register

This is a chronological list of share transfers that have occurred over time. In addition other information details like transfer number and date, details of the transferee and transferor and details of the certificate that was cancelled and the certificate that was issued are also included.

Part 2:

Money Money Money!

CHAPTER 4

Raising Capital For Your Business

When we are talking business, there is no way we can leave out money! The input and output for any business is money. So, as you gear up to fight hard to earn profits and make good money, you will also have to find the resources and entities that can fund your entry into the business. There are no two ways about the fact that no matter how economically you try to get started, you are going to need money for every milestone and every facet of your business from inception to implementation.

Simply, raising capital for a business is a three-step process. The first step for any business owner is to look for ways and sources that fund businesses. Out of all the available sources, you will need to look at sources that fund businesses similar to yours. Finally, the most important step to identify all the requirements and documents that the funding agency needs about you and your business to sanction your loan amount. It would not be wrong to say that the difference between keeping your business goals a dream and transforming them into reality lies in how well you execute these three steps.

Research the Sources

Research is the foundation of the three-step process, which we mentioned in the previous section. Unless you identify the available options correctly, you will never be able to identify the right funding options for your business needs. The required information can be accessed from online as well as offline sources. The advent of Internet has made it excessively easy to access information from around the world. There are several websites and online resources that are available for you to explore. However, one of the most important of these resources is the SBA (Small Business Administration) website, which presents all the facts and resources required by a new business owner.

Apart from the Internet, there are several offline sources available to you as well, which may be accessed by the user for additional information. The problem with some online resources, unless you access or download them from credible sources, is that their authenticity is questionable. On the other hand, offline resources are usually published under a well-known name. Therefore, they are more dependable. You may take a look at the local newspapers and visit the public library to look at some of the material that they have in this regard.

Identify the Sources

Several types of financing options exist and not all options may be for you. Therefore, it is important for you to have some basic information about the types of funding options and their relevance for your business type.

- **Equity Financing**

  In this type of financing option, the funding agency gets partial ownership in the business. The biggest advantage of opting for this type of funding option is that the owner can return the investment in fixed duration of time. Therefore, the owner can invest his or her time on the business instead of focusing on returning debts. However, the disadvantage of this arrangement is that the business owner loses full autonomy in the business.

- **Personal Funding**

  Bootstrapping or making use of your personal finances for starting a business is one of the commonest ways of generating finances for a new venture. Some of the commonly used sources of income include credit cards, savings accounts and other accounts that may be scanned for unused money. If you have a good amount of money, then you may think of funding your business without any external support.

- **Friends and Family**

  Another form of personal finances or easy money that you may return on your own basis and time is money taken from friends and family. This money is exactly like your own money with the difference that you have borrowed it from someone who trusts you and has conviction in you. So, he or she can give you the freedom and time to work on your ideas without pushing you to pay their money back.

- **Angel Investors and Venture Capitalists**

  Investors and capitalists invest in businesses via equity financing. However, you may have to pay back huge returns. Therefore, this is usually the last option that people like to explore.

- **Debt Financing**

  What is loan for a common man is debt financing for a new business owner. Banks and organizations commonly offer such loans to people who have promising business plans for the future. The advantage of using this form of financing is that bank of the source organization does not claim any stakes in the business. Therefore, the business owner is in full control of the business. However, the only disadvantage of such loans is that if a business owner has a loan on him or her, he might not be able to pool in resources from other investors and creditors.

Application for Loan

When applying for loans to start a business, there are several types of loans that a startup can avail. Some of the common business loans available in the market include start-up business loans, small-scale business loans, new business loans and large business loans. With the advent of Internet, the whole process of submitting an online application, its approval and status communication is shifted to the online platform. So, as a user, you can now apply online and make all the calculations regarding eligibility, loan amount and payment process without any problem.

How To Determine the Money You Need

Now that you already have an idea about the different sources of funding, the next thing that you need to think about is the money you need for your business. Initial expenses can be too high for some businesses in view of the fact that initial infrastructure establishment needs to be put in place. Getting the technology, office supplies, rent for office space and electricity/utility bill, employee management and marketing expenses constitute initial startup costs. Another hidden cost that forms an integral part of the startup cost is professional and legal fees.

Can Lack Of Finances Be One Of The Reasons For Failure

Failure in business may be a result of a number of factors. One of the most pioneering reasons is financial crunch or the inability to raise enough capital for running the business to the point where the business can give them the returns that they expect. In several cases, businessmen do not make the right assessment of the expenses land up being in a financial crunch. Instead of attempting to raise more funds, most businessmen limit their expenses. This indirectly limits the capacity of their business and its future in the long run.

*"I can accept Failure, everyone fails at something, But I can't accept not trying." – **Michael Jordan***

Looking Outside For Financial Help

Whenever a business owner starts a new business, he or she is mostly recommended to look for outside financial sources to not just start the business, but also sustain or revive the business. These financial sources are loans and investments from banks and friends. Don't be surprised if you have underestimated your startup cost because you are not alone. Most new business owners make this mistake. However, fortunately, there are several options for you to explore even after you have landed yourself into trouble. All you need to do is research and find the options that exist for you.

CHAPTER 5

Bookkeeping And Accounting Basics

For a new business owner, two of the most daunting tasks are bookkeeping and accounting. However, if you understand them well, they should not pose to be a problem for you. Two basic things that you need to be mindful of include:

- The first thing is to keep tab of all the expenses, earnings and profits in a detailed manner.

- The second thing is to remain mindful about the tax filing process.

Contrary to popular belief, you don't really need to organize or keep your records in any specific order. The only requirement here is that your records must be able to provide profit and expenses related information in full.

Bookkeeping, in general, is an easy process. Typically, it is a three-step process. The first thing is to maintain a clear record of all the expenditure that your business involves. You need to analyze the records to keep a tab of the expenditure and income related to your business. This should be done on a periodic basis, which may be daily, weekly, fortnightly or monthly. The third and last step in the process is to create financial reports, which shall be used to create milestones and analyze business progress regularly. Regardless of whether you choose the manual or automatic method of accounting, the principles and steps involved in bookkeeping remain the same. In this section, we shall take a deeper look at the steps involved.

Save Receipts

Every single purchase and sale that is a part of your business must be recorded in the form of a receipt, which must contain details like date, amount and all the other important information related to the transaction. It is a collection of these receipts that will help you create a transaction summary. There are several different ways in which you can create a summary of your transactions and maintain a record of the same. For instance, legally, you may keep a file of receipts or maintain a cash register. This cash register may also be maintained using computer software. However, which system to follow largely depends on the needs of the business.

For instance, if you own a small business, the transactions associated with the business will be relatively fewer in number. Therefore, it is possible to maintain a record of these transactions manually. However, as the business grows, the transactions are expected to increase in number. With the rising numbers, it may not be possible for a single person to keep tab of all the transaction and accurately prepare a summary.

Set Up

Once you have the receipts and documents ready for your expenditures, the next thing on your list should be to prepare a ledger or summary of all these transactions over a fixed period of time. This summary will answer most of your financial questions. The first part of this step is to post the receipts of your transactions to the ledger on a regular basis. Depending on the number of transactions that your business involves, you may post these receipts once a day or on a weekly/monthly basis. This process is typically referred to as posting. You can also automate this process by using accounting software for the posting and ledger creation purpose.

Create Financial Reports

No matter how much information you collect, none of it will be of any substantial use to you if you are not able to analyze them and derive meaningful information from them. For instance, unless you measure the total expenses against the income generated, you will not be able to judge if your business is making profit or is under loss. Moreover, for information like whether your credit customers are paying back on time or not, you will need to generate financial reports. All in all, you need financial reports to get a bigger picture on your business and what you can derive from the same.

CHAPTER 6

Small Business Tax Basics

While talking business, one of the most essential and basic things that you will need to look at and take special note of is tax. In fact, if you need to look at the annual tax bill for a business, you will get a good idea of how skilled and knowledgeable the owner is. Paying taxes is an extremely essential part of any business if you are hoping to run it for a long time and grow it gradually from a small business to a bigger business entity.

While you may hire a professional or expert to do the tax evaluation and payment as you grow, it is always a good idea to have some basic knowledge of the field yourself. No one knows your business better than you and no one will be willing to make savings as much as you. Therefore, your involvement in every aspect of the business can play a crucial role in the success and growth of your business.

Write Everything Down

One of the first and basic things that you need to do as a business owner is to keep a tab of the business revenue and expenses on paper. An intelligent deduction of expenses from the earning can help you reduce your taxable income by a considerable degree. Obviously, you wouldn't like to pay for the part of the income that you did not receive. Some of the common deductions include travel expenses, infrastructure costs, maintenance expenses and employee payments. In addition, depreciation and losses also need to be counted in deductions.

Employee Taxes

If your business has employees who are working for you on a permanent or contractual basis, there are several taxes that you will need to deduct from their salaries and pay to the local authorities on their behalf.

Quarterly Estimated Taxes

It is a good practice to estimate taxes on a quarterly basis to ensure that you don't fall into cash flow trouble at the end of the year with the taxes value mounting up considerably. Some of the issues that most businessmen face includes calculating the amount of tax that needs to be paid and who is liable to pay it.

Sales Tax

If you are offering any service or product, you will need to check with the local authorities if your business's offerings require you to pay a service tax. Moreover, you must get yourself registered with the local service tax department and track your sales irrespective of whether they fall under the taxable or non-taxable category.

Part 3:

Small Business Marketing 101

CHAPTER 7

Defining Your Market

There is no rocket science in the fact that if you need your business to succeed and earn you profits, then you will need to have customers who are willing to buy your products or avail the services that your business offers. Having the passion for a job is good, but unless the job is capable of earning you money, you cant really call yourself a businessman. This is perhaps the reason why one of the first things that you need to do is to define your customer base. Once you have defined your target customer list, you can focus your energies on marketing and how you can reach your word out to the market.

"You are never tool old to set another goal or to dream a new dream." – **C.S. Lewis**

Is Defining Your Market Really Important

There are no ways about the fact that knowing who your target audience is can take you a long way forward in your endeavors to achieve success in your business. To point out some specific ways in which defining a market helps a business include:

- Evaluate the potential of your business idea on the basis of whether there is a market for your products at all.

- Make the required changes in your business idea to make it suitable for your target audience.

- Streamline the marketing efforts for your business with specific attention towards a well-defined section of the market.

All in all, once you clearly define your market, you can limit and save on your marketing efforts considerably in view of the fact that you know exactly what to say in your marketing material. You know your audience and you know what will drive them towards your product. These two things are capable of getting you really far in your marketing campaign without having to give in a lot of money or efforts into the process.

Defining A Market For A Business

While defining a market for your business, you need to remember that you are basically identifying a class of people who would be interested in buying your products or availing your services. Moreover, you are doing this identification with the intention to know what these people are hoping for as far as your offerings are concerned. Therefore, you need to have a personal and demographic profile of your audience. Some of the things that you need to fill out include:

- Occupation

- Gender

- Age

- Buying habits

- Income level

- Family status in terms of family size

- Marital status

- Ethnic group

- Interests

- Political and religious views

- Geographic location

- Hobbies

From the list, it will be very clear that you need to have a detailed profile of your audience and clearly define the age group, area of belonging and background of the customers. This is what will help you decide the language, tone and message structure that you need to put across for maximum effect. In some cases, target customers or audience may be businesses. A personal profile may not be possible for them. However, basic characteristics like size, employee strength, and location and industry type are some of the important things that you need to look at.

CHAPTER 8

Learning About Your Market

Doing business successfully requires you to remain on the learning spree forever. You need to be constantly in touch with whom your customers are, competitors that exist for your services/products in the market and the industry latest.

> *"I have not failed. I've just found 10,000 ways that won't work."* **– Thomas Edison**

Market research of this kind is essential for a business owner in view of the fact that knowing products/services are in demand and predicting their fate for the future. Market research can be helpful in several ways. Some of these include:

- Identifying opportunities
- Mitigating risks

- Predicting and analyzing potential and existing industry problems.

Market research is a three-step process. As a business owner, it is important for you to have an idea about the process and what it needs from you to get the going right for your business in every respect. The following sections elaborate on the different steps and the basic sub-processes that they involve.

Identify the Sources

Research is all about data analysis and to analyze data, you need to have data. There are several sources of data that you can explore and request to get the required. One of the primary sources of data in this regard is the Government. The Government is capable of providing you information about industries, organizations and the economic conditions related to the same. Therefore, you can use this information to gain insights into which your customers and competitors are. Some of the things that you can easily know from this data source include:

- Employment Statistics

- Economic Indicators

- Earnings and Income Statistics

Identify Secondary Sources of Data

In addition to the fundamental data sources, you may also explore the allied sources of data like magazines, groups, institutions and internet-based databases. These sources can be used to find patterns and trends related to the industry.

Understand The Global Nature Of Businesses

Businesses are no longer localized or national level in nature. The businesses of today are global in every sense of the word. They thrive and grow in the international market and this is perhaps the reason why you need to understand that no matter how small your business mat be, international factors and the happenings in the international market have a significant role to play in your business and how well it works for you.

CHAPTER 9

Building Your Website And Social Media

The advent if Internet has led to the rise of the use of social media and online presence in how business connects with its target audience and markets its products and services. In fact, a recent survey has shown that the use of online presence and social media can help a business rise faster by as much as 40%.

*"Extraordinary performance is possible only through extraordinary preparation." – **Darren Hardy***

There are two basic things that your business needs to have if you are hoping to create an online identity for it – website and social media business page. For either of these options, it is a good idea to get started with registering your domain and read on.

Social Media Presence

One of the easiest ways to have an online identity is to redirect your domain name to your business social media page. While simplicity and cost effectiveness are the two most profound advantages of using this method, it also offers you an added advantage of increased credibility and trust. When a business says, 'follow me on Facebook', the user instantly relates to it. Therefore, you can expect a higher level of engagement for your business.

In addition, establishing social media presence can be a critical part of your branding plan. As a business owner, you have options galore as far as choosing the right social platform for your business is concerned. Some of these options include Facebook, Google+, Twitter and LinkedIn. You can choose the platform that you are most comfortable with.

Although, it is quick, easy, affordable and effective, this method suffers from some basic issues like lack of ownership and the compulsion of operating on an open forum. Moreover, you can customize your presence only to a specific level and the tools available to you are also limited. A quick word of advice here is that you must never try to conquer everything at once. Go one step at a time and follow a plan.

Having A Website

If your business has a website of its own, then you have a sure shot tool for reaching out to your customers as a brand. There are several free and paid options available to you in this regard and you can either go for the professionally made, completely customized website or use one of the free options to create a basic one. The immense popularity of platforms like Wordpress and Joomla has made it excessively easy to people who wish to use a drag-and-drop platform for designing their websites on their own.

Apart from being the entity that will represent your business in the online space, a website also allows complete ownership and reduces overhead costs in the sense that your customers can easily look at your company information online. Moreover, it allows you the flexibility to design, project and promote your business in the manner that you desire. So, you can choose the design of every single page, the images that will be displayed and every bit of text that will be there on your website. With that said, it is surely a complex system to design, implement and maintain. So, if you can deal with the complexities that come with it, a website is a bare essential for any business.

CHAPTER 10

Writing A Press Release

When it comes to adverting your business, one of the first tools that you will need to have is a press release. It can be one of the most effective things on your advertising documents list if you take the time and invest the energy required to write it correctly. Before anything else, you need to understand that what a press release is. Simply, a piece of text that is floated in the media to put the word across about your business is called a press release or a news release.

Writing a press release requires you to follow some basic steps, which have been illustrated below.

- **Create a Catchy Title**

    The first thing that your press release needs to have is a catchy title. The title is the headline of your release document and should be attractive enough to gather the attention of your audience towards it instantly. Typically, this title should not be more than 20 words long.

- **Write a Summary**

The next thing that your press release needs to have is a summary. Ideally, it must not exceed a couple of lines. Pitching in a quote or a line that best describes your business here can just be what you need.

- **Mention the Date and Place**

Generally, the publishing unit will generate the time and location automatically. However, it is a good idea to put it in the release document before submitting.

- **Identify the Five Ws**

The first paragraph of the release must be able to answer the five Ws right away. The text must be cleverly planned to describe clearly the 'what, who, where, what and when'.

- **Add a Testimonial Statement**

  The press release is the first document about your business that will be rolled out to the public. In view of this, you need to ensure that your press release is credible. Therefore, it is a good idea to put a statement from someone important in the business, which gives the reader an idea about the intention, goal and purpose of the business.

- **Describe Your Business**

  In the remaining part of the press release, you need to reiterate all the important things about the business that you customers and potential customers must know.

- **Call-to-Action**

  It is essential to leave the press release on a note that states where the reader can find more information about your business or contact you.

Part 4:

Small Business Resources

Website resources for Small Businesses

http://allbusiness.com

http://businessweek.com

http://sba.gov

http://irs.gov

http://entrepreneur.com

http://marketwatch.com

http://wsj.com

https://www.americanexpress.com/us/small-business/shop-small/

Video Resources for Small Businesses

https://www.youtube.com/watch?v=h-VA8IZhZeI

https://www.youtube.com/watch?v=3OhgivN9YQY

https://www.youtube.com/watch?v=GS04yv4xgpE

https://www.youtube.com/watch?v=aMIESSL6W6o

Small Business Startup resources

https://www.score.org/

http://www.coordinatedlegal.com/SecretaryOfState.html

Win a Brand-New 6.6 inch Kindle Fire HD

Open to residents in the U.S., Australia, Canada, England, Europe and India

As part of the launch of Our New Bull City publishing Series, I'm giving away a brand-new Kindle Fire HD this month. Somebody reading this post will win. The contest is only open to fans and readers who are on my opt-in list.

Here's the deal. Any Customer that downloads one of our books, writes a nice testimonial, AND places the review on Amazon, you will then be entered into raffle to win a 6.6 inch Kindle Fire HD. The odds of you winning are better than the lottery. I'm thinking only twenty people will actually post a review by the end of the month. If that holds true, you would have a one in twenty chance of winning. That's great odds.

I will take all of the testimonials from Amazon, posted from the 5th, through the 30th of the month, put them in a jar, and randomly pull out a winner. The winner will be announced on the 1st of every month, in an email like this one. The brand-new Kindle Fire will be shipped to your door, whether you live in the U.S., Canada, Australia, England, Europe, or India. Again, all you have to do is purchase one of our Books between now and the 30th and place a review on Amazon by that time.

Why am I giving away a free Kindle Fire? Many reviews of a book help readers to discover new books, and everyone loves to find fresh authors previously unknown to them. Many four and five star reviews will help to validate that our book.

If you're willing to help me and want to win a 6.6 inch Kindle Fire HD, Simply post your Honest review and email me a link of your review to info@bullcitypublishing.com with Kindle Raffle in the Subject line

Thank You for Your Purchase!!!!!

B U L L C I T Y
P U B L I S H I N G

Thank you again for ordering this book!

I hope this book was able to provide you with the Information that you were searching for. Lastly, if you REALLY enjoyed this book, then I'd like to ask you for a favor, would you be kind enough to leave a review for this book on Amazon? It'd be greatly appreciated!

Lastly, Please be sure to connect with us We Would Love to Hear from You

Bull City Publishing Social Media Links:

Blog: http://bullcitypublishing.com/blog/

Facebook Group:
https://www.facebook.com/groups/bullcitypublishing/

Twitter: https://twitter.com/BullCityPub

Instagram: http://instagram.com/bullcitypublishing

Pintrest: https://pintrest.com/bullcitypub

Linkedin: http://www.linkedin.com/companies/5311112

Tumblr: http://bullcitypublishing.tumblr.com

Do you Love Reading? Do you want a Ton of FREE Kindle Books? Join our Mailing list by emailing us at freebooks@bullcitypublishing.com

Do you Need Help Writing a Book? Would you like to get published? If So Shoot us an email publish@bullcitypublishing.com or Visit http://bullcitypublishing.com/get-published/

Thank you and good luck!

James Moore

Check Out My Other Books

Below you'll find some of my other popular books that are popular on Amazon and Kindle as well. Simply click on the links below to check them out.

http://www.amazon.com/How-Start-Successful-Hair-Salon-ebook/dp/B00ED8F7EO

http://www.amazon.com/Opening-Boutique-Guide-Clothing-Starting-ebook/dp/B00EOAVAN8

http://www.amazon.com/Becoming-coupon-Warrior-Extreme-couponing-ebook/dp/B00LO8KCBY

http://www.amazon.com/Online-Marketing-Real-Estate-Professionals-ebook/dp/B00EF5DTH2

http://www.amazon.com/How-Read-Body-Language-101-ebook/dp/B00HBUA35E

http://www.amazon.com/Clothing-Line-Start-Guide-Successful-ebook/dp/B00EEWE0PQ

http://www.amazon.com/How-Start-Rap-Record-Label-ebook/dp/B00EE6RAOA

http://www.amazon.com/Hip-Hop-Rhyming-Dictionary-Extensive-ebook/dp/B00FF8SDZ6

http://www.amazon.com/Start-African Restaurant -Without-Losing-Shirt-ebook/dp/B00EETB6Y2

http://www.amazon.com/Play-Piano-Fast-Yourself-Playing-ebook/dp/B00LUQ1SKO

http://www.amazon.com/Fashion-Show-Secrets-guide-fashion-ebook/dp/B00LUPNPTW

62595364R00041

Made in the USA
Lexington, KY
12 April 2017